First Facts®

Transportation Zone

Police Cars

in Action

by Becky Olien

CAPSTONE PRESS
a capstone imprint

First Facts is published by Capstone Press,
151 Good Counsel Drive, P.O. Box 669, Mankato, Minnesota 56002.
www.capstonepub.com

Books published by Capstone Press are manufactured with paper
containing at least 10 percent post-consumer waste.

Library of Congress Cataloging-in-Publication Data
Olien, Rebecca.
  Police cars in action/by Becky Olien.
     p. cm.—(First facts. Transportation zone)
  Includes bibliographical references and index.
  ISBN 978-1-4296-6825-5 (library binding)
  1. Police vehicles—Juvenile literature. I. Title.
  HV7936.V4O553 2012
  363.2'32—dc22   2010054615

Editorial Credits

Karen L. Daas and Anthony Wacholtz, editors; Gene Bentdahl, designer; Eric Gohl,
    media researcher; Laura Manthe, production specialist

Image Credits

Capstone Studio/Jim Foell, 6; Karon Dubke, 14, 17, 18, 22
Dreamstime/Firebrandphotography, 1
Getty Images Inc./Popperfoto, 10
Library of Congress, 9
Shutterstock/Brad Sauter, 13; Paul Matthew Photography, cover; SVLuma, 21
SuperStock Inc./Ron Brown, 5

Printed in the United States of America in North Mankato, Minnesota.

032011   006110CGF11

Table of Contents

Police Cars

They're loud, fast, and on the streets to help. Police cars zoom into action to keep people safe. You see police cars as they **patrol** neighborhoods. You see them on the scene of accidents and emergencies. Police cars help officers do their jobs.

patrol: to travel around an area to protect it or to watch over people

Police Officers

Police officers work hard to keep people safe. They help people who are hurt or lost. Officers make sure people follow laws. They sometimes write tickets to people who break laws. They also direct traffic at accidents.

Before Police Cars

Before cars were invented, police officers rode horses or walked. They used paddy wagons to carry people who were arrested. Paddy wagons are no longer used, but some officers still use horses today.

9

Early Police Cars

The first police cars were much simpler than modern police cars. Police officers began using cars in the early 1900s. By the 1930s, police cars had a few extra lights. An officer turned a crank to sound the **siren**. Most police officers drove police cars instead of riding horses.

siren: a machine that makes a loud noise

Parts of a Police Car

Today's police cars have more parts than earlier models. Each part of a police car has a job to do. Flashing lights on the light bar warn other drivers to get out of the way. Spotlights are used to light up dark places. Glass or metal separates the back seat from the front. A camera records what happens in front of the car.

light bar

camera

spotlight

engine

How a Police Car Works

Police cars work much like cars you see every day. The **engine** powers the car. The accelerator speeds up the car. The brake slows it down. The steering wheel turns the car. Switches control the car's lights and sirens.

engine: a machine that makes the power needed to move something

Equipment

Police cars store equipment that helps officers do their job. First-aid kits allow officers to help people who are hurt. Police officers use fire extinguishers to put out fires at accidents. Radios keep the officers in contact with one another.

18

Police Cars Today

Police cars are equipped to help officers in many situations. Laptop computers allow police officers to write reports and get information fast. A **GPS** shows directions so the officers know where to go. Police cars also have equipment to measure other cars' speeds.

GPS: an electronic tool used to find the location of an object

Police Car Facts

- Police cars are also called squad cars and cruisers.

- Police officers practice driving on test tracks. They learn to take sharp corners while driving fast. They also learn how to drive on wet, slippery roads.

- Police officers use their cars as an office. They have everything they need to do reports or talk with other officers.

- Police cars flash red and blue lights during an emergency. They sometimes use white and yellow lights for nonemergency situations, such as directing traffic.

Some police cars look like other cars on the street. These cars have sirens and lights hidden in the car's grille. Police officers use these unmarked cars to catch people who are speeding. They are also used for undercover work.

Hands On: Make a Siren

Police car sirens are loud so that people can hear them above other sounds. The loudspeaker is the part of the siren that makes sound louder.

What You Need

scissors
wax paper
plastic cup
rubber band

paper towel
cardboard tube
your voice
an adult to help

What You Do

1. Cut a square of wax paper to fit over the open end of the plastic cup.
2. Use the rubber band to hold the wax paper in place.
3. Ask an adult to cut off the bottom end of the plastic cup.
4. Wrap a folded paper towel around the cardboard tube.
5. Push the cardboard tube into the bottom of the plastic cup.
6. Make siren noises into the open end of the tube.

Sounds are made by vibrations. Feel the wax paper move when you make sounds. The tube and cup make your voice louder. Loud police car sirens warn people to get out of the way.

Glossary

accelerator (ak-SEL-uh-ray-tor)—the pedal used to speed up a car

brake (BRAKE)—the pedal used to slow down or stop a car

emergency (i-MUR-juhn-see)—a sudden situation that must be handled quickly

engine (EN-juhn)—a machine that makes the power needed to move something

GPS (JEE PEE ESS)—an electronic tool used to find the location of an object; GPS stands for global positioning system

grille (GRIL)—an opening that allows air to cool the engine of a car

patrol (puh-TROHL)—to travel around an area to protect it or to keep watch over people

siren (SYE-ruhn)—a machine that makes a loud noise; police cars have sirens to warn people to get out of the way

Read More

Armentrout, David, and Patricia Armentrout. *The Police Station*. Our Community. Vero Beach, Fla.: Rourke Pub., 2009.

Gonzalez, Lissette. *Police in Action*. Dangerous Jobs. New York: PowerKids Press, 2008.

Internet Sites

FactHound offers a safe, fun way to find Internet sites related to this book. All of the sites on FactHound have been researched by our staff.

Here's all you do:

Visit *www.facthound.com*

Type in this code: 9781429668255

Check out projects, games and lots more at
www.capstonekids.com

Index